GRACE-WORDS

"Words of hope, inspiration, encouragement, and challenge."

*Brie –
Run Under
God's grace!
Stie Amazed!
Chris*

CHRIS A. GILLESPIE

Copyright © 2015 by Chris A. Gillespie

Published by TEAM 413 – GRACERUNNER MINISTRIES

Photos by Friends of TEAM 413

Printed & Bound by TransAmerica Printing
Birmingham, Alabama

Dedicated to my family...

I am blessed beyond measure to love and to be loved without condition.

FOREWORD

I'm so excited Chris has put together a collection of his motivational GRACE-WORDS. I start my day with GRACE-WORDS, letting the words fill my heart and infuse my soul. Many days, when I need a boost, I'll sign into Facebook to read a message again. Now, with this wonderful book, I'll be able to pick up and read a motivational thought exactly when I need it. GRACE-WORDS is a book you can enjoy every day all year long. Read it one page at a time, one day at a time, or open it randomly and let Chris' words inspire your day, encourage you, or motivate you.

Lisa Belcastro
Award-winning Author of inspirational Fiction

GRACE-WORDS brings out the absolute best in what living a life of grace and dignity mean. I have seen this first hand by watching and following Chris for several years. Chris "practices what he preaches" and inspires me each day more than he will ever know.

A self-made man struggles to give God the glory for his accomplishments, but the grace-made man never forgets to give Christ the credit for his success. Grace brings out the best in humble hearts. Look for the love in their eyes!

Lisa Smith-Batchen
Coach - Motivational Speaker - Endurance athlete

PREFACE

In 2010 I began writing GRACE-WORDS on our TEAM 413 social media sites as a way to connect with our worldwide audience. More than five years later the simple words that God has given to this simple man have reached and touched hundreds of thousands of lives. I am truly humbled and honored to be God's messenger through GRACE-WORDS.

I thank God each day for allowing me to be His servant through this wonderful gift of His amazing grace. My prayer is that God will use these words to plant hope and inspiration deep within your soul and will encourage and challenge you to accomplish far more than you ever thought possible.

Under HIS Grace,

Chris A. Gillespie
Founder & Executive Director
TEAM 413 – GRACERUNNER MINISTRIES

"While God did not give me a life void of sadness, free of pain, and without tough times – I have always felt His goodness in my life. I have been given a life of enduring joy because God rescued me through Jesus Christ."

"Never allow your circumstances to dictate your character. Instead, allow your faith to show through so others will see Christ in you!"

"During the tough times of life when you don't believe that you can keep going — God remains your best choice."

"Taking a risk in order to accomplish something extraordinary is much better than sitting back and doing nothing because you fear failure. God teaches lessons through the step by step process of moving forward. That's success! That's strength! That's grace!"

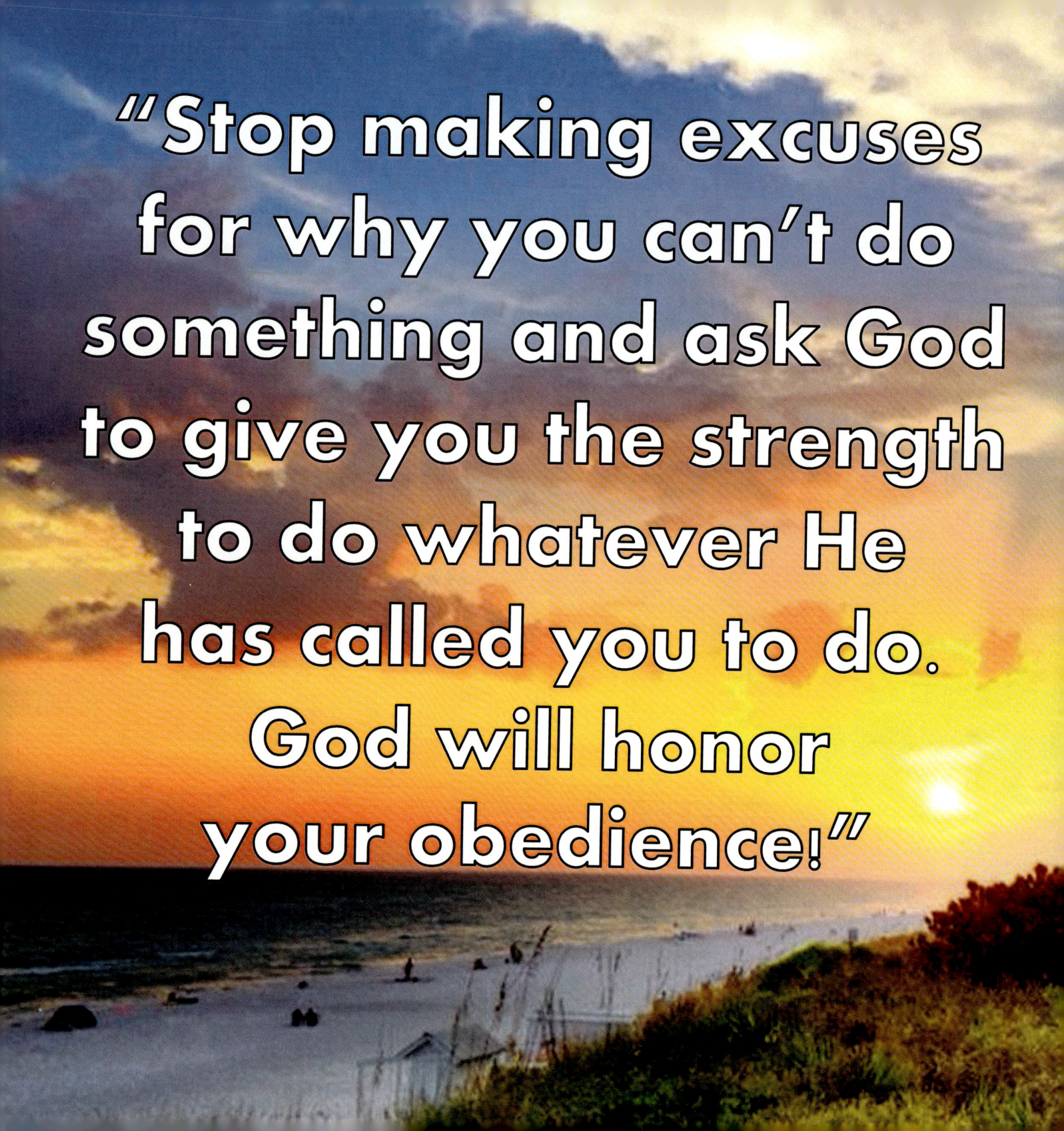

"Stop making excuses for why you can't do something and ask God to give you the strength to do whatever He has called you to do. God will honor your obedience!"

"Unlike people of this world, God will never write you off or minimize you as if you had no feelings. He loves you regardless of what you've done. He will come to you wherever you are. He will always give more grace! You can count on Him!"

"The foundation of my life is not dependent on the things of this world, but grounded in my relationship with my Lord and Savior, Jesus Christ."

"Why would you compromise your faith and give in to the things of this world when you have the knowledge that Christ NEVER compromised grace for you?"

"Tough times in life should NEVER cause us to ignore the sovereignty of God!"

"None of us are qualified or worthy to be servants of God. Yet, if we humble ourselves before Him and lay our ALL down at His feet, He can use us to do amazing things for His Kingdom and for His glory!"

"Sometimes losing something that you believe you can't live without is God's way of reminding you that you can't go through life without Him!"

"It's amazing what you can accomplish when you draw strength from being held in the powerful grip of God's grace."

"Be a blessing to someone today for yesterday is gone and tomorrow is yet to be."

"Being strong is sometimes best described through our greatest weakness. For when we are at the bottom looking up, God can use us so that others may see the depth of His love for us. When we are at the bottom, we become completely dependent upon Him and that's exactly where He wants us to be!"

"When the tears you shed hit the ground because there is no shoulder to cry on - When no one understands and you feel all alone - When the pain is so searing and so deep that you hurt to the core of your soul - Remember that God is there! He loves you and will hear you call out for help."

"Change is inevitable. How you deal with it is a reflection of God's presence in your life."

"It doesn't matter who you are, where you have been, or what you have done – God loves you and has a plan for your life."

"Failure is an opportunity to achieve a dream left unfinished. Others are watching to see how you will respond when you trip and fall. Allow God to use your shortcoming as a window to your soul so others will see Christ in you."

"In my weakest times when I thought I couldn't go on, when the silence of the night was deafening, and through times so dark that I couldn't see my way out -- God has never left me! He has never given up on me!"

"Loving and caring for others is an outward manifestation of God at work in your life."

"It is inconceivable to me how anyone can go through the tough times of life without a relationship with God and trusting Him with the promise that all things work together for good for those who love Him and have been called to His purpose."

"We were created to serve God. And when we do, a lot of that other stuff just doesn't matter anymore!"

"Don't waste the gifts of each breath and every heartbeat. Look to God for guidance and move swiftly in the direction of His calling."

"Christians invest their lives, talent, and finances in many things. One simple rule should be followed when making those decisions – Is there a positive eternal impact for the cause of Christ?"

"Life would be much better, less complex, and filled with more joy if before making a decision we asked one simple question – Would God approve?"

"Your hope is in **CHRIST** alone! Broken, battered, bruised, torn, tattered, discounted, dismissed, and ridiculed by this world? He loves you **REGARDLESS**! Treasure **HIM** for **HE** treasures you!"

Dedication, patience, determination, toughness, willpower, motivation, relentlessness, guts, and grit are just a few of the characteristics that a runner must have to get the job done – to press and push the pace. Yet, as a Christian we need these attributes to move forward in life and finish the race that God has blessed and entrusted to us."

"It is a sign of strength when you stand by your faith in God and refuse to compromise your beliefs even though the world says you should."

"Time is fleeting. Years, months, days, and hours fly by. Yet, the mercy, grace, and love of God through Christ never end. He has never let me down. He gives me enduring unconditional love. He is always with me and He fills my days with great joy through my family and friends. For this and the many blessings in my life, I give Him praise!"

"God offers opportunities for us to serve Him through loving people, helping causes, sowing seeds, and sharing our faith forward. It's our responsibility to get the job done."

"God can see gifts and talents in us that we cannot see ourselves. Even in our doubt – In spite of our unbelief – He never gives up on us. For this gift of abounding love and many other reasons, we should never give up on Him by giving in to the things of this world!"

"The bottom line --- If you are a Christian, God has called you to influence the world in which you live for Jesus Christ!"

"The marathon of life is a culmination of effort driven by a force deep within. For some that force is something of this world and it once was for me as well. Now, my steps are motivated by Christ who gives me the strength to move forward under His grace and for that, I am still amazed!"

"What you are willing to walk away from determines what God will bring to you!"

"God's timing is always perfect. He knows what is best and He reveals the beauty of His grace in ways that we could never imagine. Allowing Him to work through us brings change to the world. Laying our all at the foot of the cross of Jesus is what He wants from us. When we give it up, extraordinary things happen and our lives will never be the same again."

"You have to go through IT to know that you can endure IT! God will be with you every step of the way."

"TODAY, look forward to discovering what God has already planned and yet to reveal!"

"God will not always give you what you want, but will provide you with what <u>HE</u> needs!"

"Despite the pain that I have endured in my life, I would never go back in time and change anything. God used the obstacles and trials of my journey to help others in ways that I cannot comprehend. For this and so much more, I give Him praise."

"When you allow others to be used by God to keep you moving in the right direction, walls of weakness, despair, regret, and guilt can crash to the ground. Accountability reveals a heart that is transparent and a soul that is set free through God's amazing grace!"

"When life is hard, remember that God loves you and you are important to Him. Pray for guidance and take the next step."

"God did not choose to give me the physical skills to be a champion in sports. However, He did give me the heart of an athlete. He gave me the will to reach for my goals. He gave me the determination to keep after the challenge at hand. He gave me guts and grit. He placed within me a burning desire, a fire deep within, to compete. More importantly, He gave me the attitude of "*team*" and for this and so much more, I praise Him!"

"If God is calling you to lead others, don't question if you are qualified. Just LEAD and He will take care of the rest."

"The likelihood of you doing something extraordinary in your life without significant sacrifice is impossible. God will give you the strength but, YOU must supply the effort. Keep plugging away ---- The impossible will become a reality when HIS strength and YOUR effort collide!"

"Throw your fears down! Throw away the chains that bind you! Rid yourself of the things that hold you captive to a life of despair. Place your ALL – your everything at the foot of the cross of Christ and let it go! You will be able to accomplish things that once seemed impossible. God will draw strength from the depths of your soul that you never knew existed!"

"Your desire to be more like Jesus is determined by the effort that you give!"

"It's been said that God will never place more on us than we can handle. I don't believe this to be totally true unless we depend on our brothers and sisters in Christ. We all need others to help us as we deal with the trails of life. Reach out your hand and heart to help someone today!"

"Look for an opportunity to help someone today. Pain of the heart is not always evident on the exterior. The sympathy, empathy, and compassion exemplified by Christ go a long way to help another heal their heart."

"Expect much to happen in your life that you won't understand. Depend on God to show you how to circumvent the obstacles that are thrown in your path. You will be better for it on the other side!"

"Run under His grace today. If it is a marathon of running or of life, stay tuned in to God's presence. In the times of trouble or of celebration, praise Him in ALL things! Let everything that has breath praise the Lord for He is worthy of your praise!"

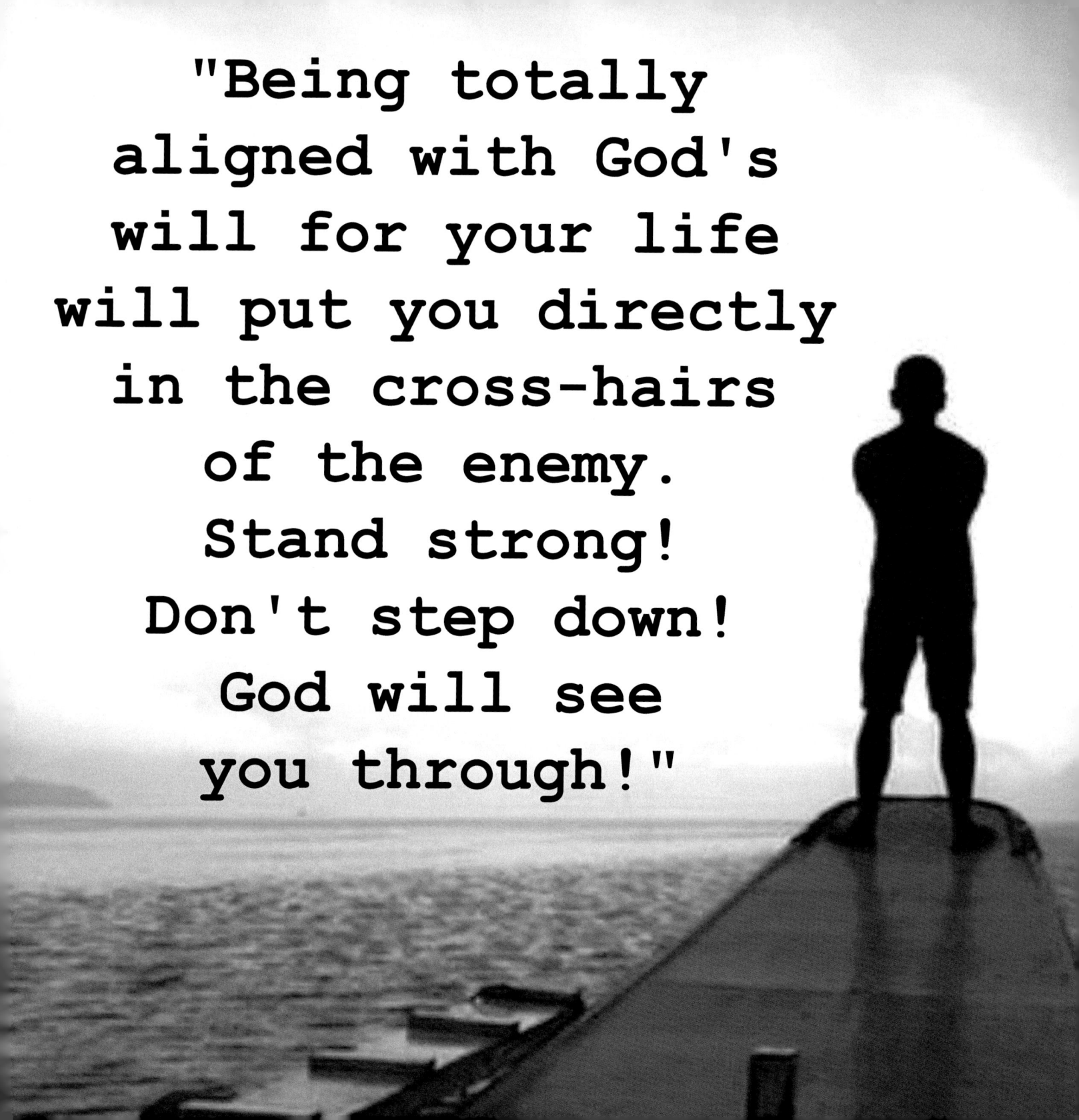

"Being totally aligned with God's will for your life will put you directly in the cross-hairs of the enemy. Stand strong! Don't step down! God will see you through!"

"Submitting to God's calling in your life takes much courage. Yet, He wouldn't ask you to do something unless you were uniquely qualified for the task. Step forward and give it your ALL — He will give you the strength and resolve to finish the drill for His glory!"

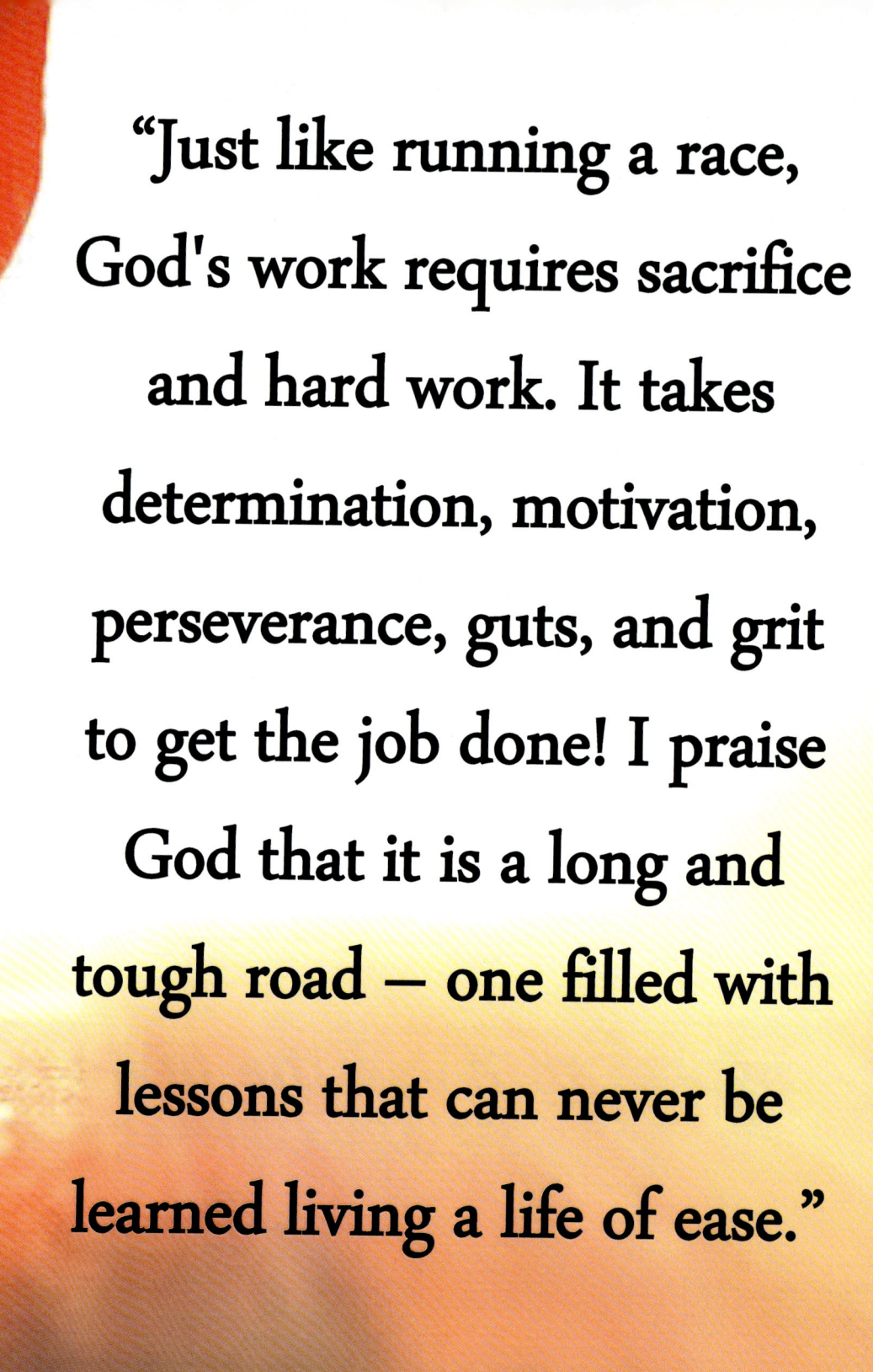

"Just like running a race, God's work requires sacrifice and hard work. It takes determination, motivation, perseverance, guts, and grit to get the job done! I praise God that it is a long and tough road — one filled with lessons that can never be learned living a life of ease."

"Use THIS day to show grace to someone in need. Make THIS the day that will change their life forever. Ensure that on THIS day Christ is so evident in your life that He cannot be ignored."

"To accomplish great things for the cause of Christ, we cannot allow mediocrity to hold us captive. It is impossible to serve Him if we are living in a ditch of comfort, self pity, or defeat!"

"While I am thankful for all of the gifts and blessings in my life, the greatest of them all is God's grace through Jesus Christ, my Savior. It cannot be bought, there is no return policy, one size fits ALL, and most importantly – When I accepted this gift, I was promised eternal life."

"When your hopes and dreams collide with God's grace, His will for your life becomes very real — it becomes so vibrant that you can see it — it becomes so tangible that you can touch it. The depth of that reality is so significant that you can never ignore it!"

"I am so thankful for 'accidental' intersections with God's amazing grace. Those times are constant reminders of His relentless pursuit of my heart."

"Our greatest strength can be our weakness. Yet, our greatest weakness can be our strength. That's where God wants us to be. Then, we are totally dependent upon HIM!"

"Living under God's grace is a blessing far greater than you can ever imagine. His unmerited favor is a gift that has already been given through Jesus Christ .... All you have to do is accept the gift of our Savior and your life will never be the same again."

"We don't have to be in a church building to worship. Worship can happen in the middle of your day – during a run – during a quiet moment – while sharing with someone else – in the midst of a troubled time. Take time to praise God today through true worship."

"Regardless of the circumstances, trials, or troubles in your life, when you refuse to communicate with a brother or sister in Christ, you have minimized God! No one is too busy or important to reach out to someone in need! Imagine if God refused to listen to your prayers."

"If you BELIEVE that God created Heaven and Earth, how can you NOT BELIEVE that He is calling you to do something that will glorify Him?"

"When things don't go as you planned or as you had wished, remember that God has never made a mistake!"

"When you allow your YESTERDAYS to dictate what happens to you TODAY, you can never move on to TOMORROW. Look for God's guidance and live TODAY for HIS glory! HIS plan for TOMORROW will fall into place when you let go and give HIM your all!"

"A simple mind cannot comprehend the strength and resolve of a heart full of faith — of a life blessed by God's grace."

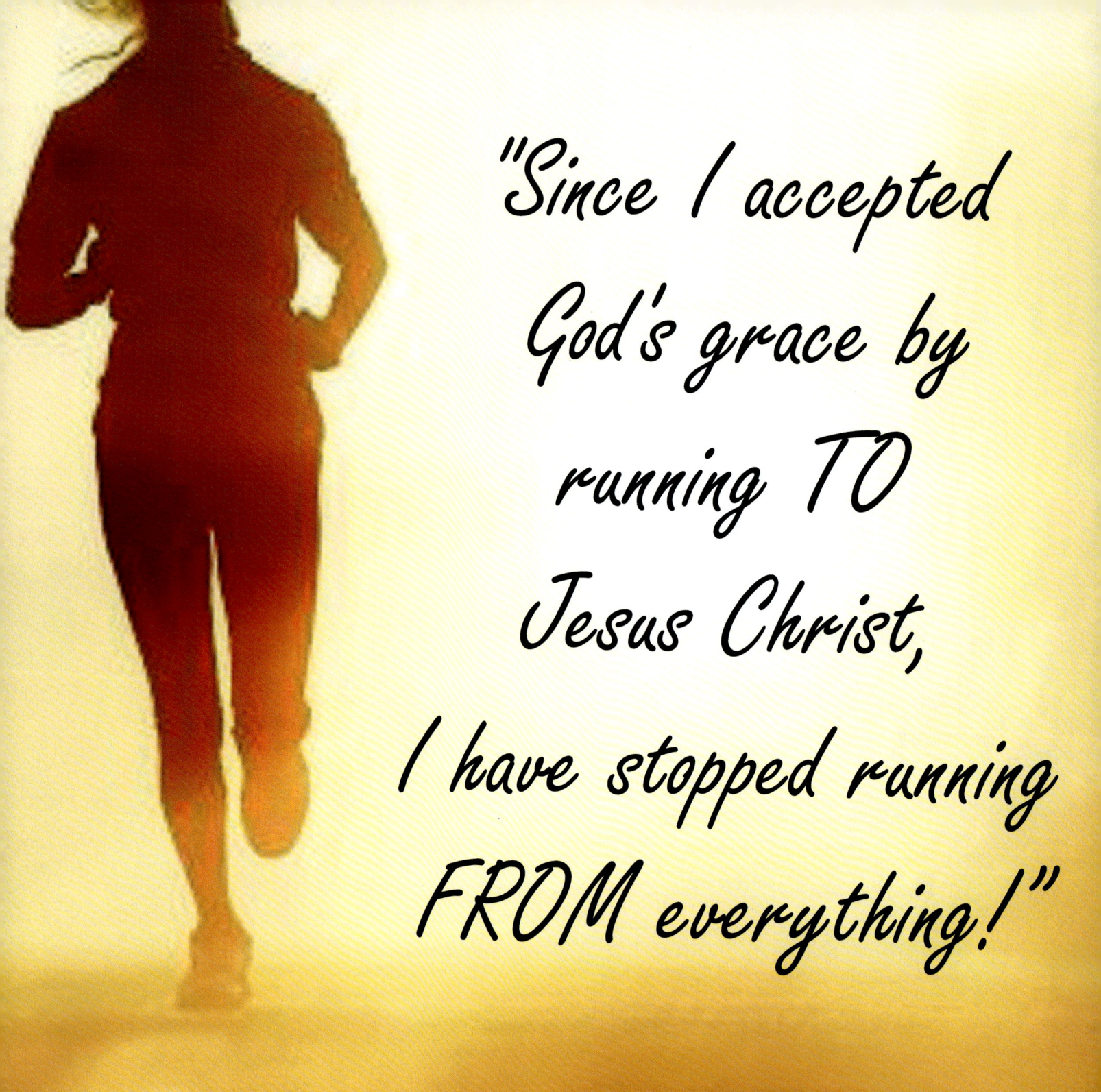

"Since I accepted God's grace by running TO Jesus Christ, I have stopped running FROM everything!"

"Share your FAITH forward by doing something to help someone today. You may lighten a burden that will change their life forever."

"If your life is filled with fear and doubt, make the decision to change. Fill your heart with praise to the Lord. You will be amazed at the difference in your own heart and in those around you."

"Praise God for burdens that eventually become a personal blessing and then help others to see and feel His love through us."

"When we allow the YESTERDAYS of life to consume us, TODAY soon becomes just another YESTERDAY and we continue the cycle of always living in the past rather than living TODAY for the glory of God."

"Sometimes I wish that I had an answer to why people go through struggles, tough times, trials, pain, and sorrow on this earth. But because I don't, I simply have to trust that God knows best even when I don't understand."

"Today someone will be watching you to see how you will respond to a circumstance, a situation, a moment of adversity, or a life trial. Will they see Christ in you?"

"Hitting the wall in a marathon is one of the toughest things that one can ever experience as an athlete. Yet, it pales in comparison to hitting the wall in life if you don't have a relationship with Jesus Christ. Through HIM you can knock down the barriers that block you from reaching the finish line standing tall!"

"In times of life when you feel all alone, remember that God has never left you. Pray – Simply talk to Him. Trust Him – He loves you!"

"God expects much from you. He may call you to do something outside your comfort zone or convict you because of your life choices, but He will never play with your emotions like some people in your life. Most of all, He will always love you without condition."

"When God calls you to do His work and you step out in faith to follow Him, remember that on the other side of circumstances that come your way, pain that you may endure, and ridicule from those who just don't understand – it will always be WORTH IT in the end!"

"Living a life based on faith in Jesus Christ has always given me hope to face the circumstances of life. I cannot imagine facing those same obstacles without Him."

"I am thankful for the beacons of hope, authors of inspiration, and examples of strength along my journey. These wonderful people have always been a constant reminder of the grace of God in my life."

"I am convinced that nothing in this world can steal your joy if you invest the totality of your life in Jesus Christ as your Lord and Savior! While you may go through trials and times of trouble and your human heart may hurt, no one can steal your joy! That's cause for celebration – that's the goodness and grace of God!"

"Never let anyone tell you that you can't do something if you believe that God is calling you to step to the front of the line!"

"Sometimes God works in ways that we don't understand. That's where faith and trust step in and we must realize that His plan is far greater than anything that we can comprehend."

"No matter the weather patterns that may pass through your day today, God wants it to be a *cobalt blue sky day* in your heart!"

"I ran away from Him because I wanted to do things on my own until I came to the realization that Jesus Christ was the answer. So, I ran to Him and now I see life through the eyes of my soul and not the eyes of this world."

"Serving God is more than just giving your time. It's an investment of your heart – it's showing the love of Christ to those who may experience His presence for the first time."

"I must be made weak to become strong. I must be knocked down to get back up. I must be at the bottom in order to look up. But, I can rest assured that Christ has already won the battle -- The enemy has been defeated. My prayer is that His work is so evident in my life that it now defines me!"

"If we dedicated as much time toward doing God's work as we spend on things that have no lasting impact at all, imagine what a difference we would make in this world!"

"You can do anything that God has given you the ability to do. If you don't think you can, you have placed self imposed limitations on your God ordained life."

"Don't run from the storms of life. Run to God for guidance."

"Wisdom is achieved through the memories of dreams attained and hopes lost. Yet, wisdom remains as evidence of God's goodness and grace!"

"God's ending to our life stories will always glorify Him. If not, we have written our own selfish endings."

"Real joy cannot be measured by the things that we personally accomplish, but by what we do for others because of the influence of Jesus Christ in our lives."

"There is NO ONE in this world who is worth coming between you and Jesus Christ."

"TODAY, look forward to discovering what God has already planned and yet to reveal!"

"Allow God to work through you by loving others. After all, when it comes to matters of the heart, it's the heart that matters."

"In the deepest, darkest recesses of your struggles in life God is there. No matter the trial, regardless of the circumstance, despite the doubt – He is there and has promised never to leave you. Even in your moment of unbelief, BELIEVE His words by trusting Him."

"When you are facing a difficult decision in life, pray and move forward. God's grace is sufficient to see you through."

"Are you running to something that is unattainable or from something that you can't outrun? Jesus Christ is the answer to all of your needs. Regardless, if you are running a real or mythical marathon in your life, He will be there with you all along your journey. Call on Him because He is all you need!"

"GOD PLANNED THIS DAY TO BE A PART OF YOUR LIFE. STOP LIVING FOR THE FUTURE AND LIVE TODAY FOR HIS GLORY!"

"When your heart becomes moldable because of the trials that you face, GOD can create a masterpiece in your life through His love, mercy, and grace – After all, your life would be a blank canvas without Him!"

"Allowing God to direct you requires FAITH strong enough to know that even if there is no path ahead, He will make a way."

"Through Jesus Christ a single ray of hope can ignite a fire within that cannot be quenched. Let Him shine through you!"

"When you tell someone that you will pray for them you have made a promise to speak to God on their behalf. Those are serious words not to be taken lightly. If you say it, do it. Someone is counting on you."

"Sometimes running is easy, sometimes it's hard, and sometimes it is just drudgery! Yet, we keep running! And, so it should be with life. God never promised a life of ease. He never promised that everything would go exactly as you want it to go. He promised to be there with you all along the way. If it is easy, hard, or drudgery, keep moving forward under His grace. He is with you!"

"I have been so blessed by the things that have happened in my life. While I didn't always understand, God had a plan and it was far greater than my own."

"When I catch myself trying to understand why God allows things to happen, I simply need to stop and realize that He is in complete control. Quite frankly, all I need to comprehend is that He is God!"

"The world may tell us that we should be afraid. God tells us to trust Him!"

"Allow God to change you from who you were yesterday to the person He wants you to be today!"

"Passion is God's heartbeat planted in your soul! If you feel it, God has something extremely important in store for you. Listen and feel for that passion .... It's God's gift to you!"

"God will give you the strength through Christ - but, you have to supply the effort. You can accomplish the seemingly impossible with this wonderful gift of His amazing grace."

"There comes a time in your training when you are climbing a huge hill and you wonder if it is worth it!
Then, you line up at the start line of a race and you know you are ready. You cross the finish line and you are thankful for those tough days. So, in life when the hill of the moment is long and steep, remember that God is preparing you to do something for His glory. You'll be ready to start and finish the plans that God has for you! That hill was a gift!"

"Failure is an opportunity to achieve a dream left unfinished. Others are watching to see how you will respond when you trip and fall. Allow God to use your shortcoming as a window to your soul so others will see Christ in you."

"Running has become so much more than an athletic endeavor for me. It is a time of worship – my quiet time with God – a time of reflection – a prayer opportunity with no outside distractions. Running is much more than it once was to me because God used it to improve the vision of the eyes of my heart."

"Grasp the pain of the endeavor and relish it – embrace it – savor it! For through the pain, God will allow you to grow whether your endeavor is athletic or personal! The pain will not last, but the accomplishment of pushing through the circumstances will give you hope and strength for the future!"

"Some of the most significant moments in my life have come when God "tapped" me on my shoulder to heal my heart! Those times are subtle reminders that even in His sovereignty, He loves and cares for me. I am so humbled by His unmerited favor – His amazing grace!"

"You can always do more than you think you can! This is true in your personal and professional life. But, with strength through Jesus Christ, you can do far more than you could ever imagine. When you give your ALL to Him, you can accomplish anything that is within His will for your life."

"Real friends don't run away from you when the walls of life are crumbling, when trouble strikes, and during the tough times. They turn around and run back to you and stay with you along the journey ahead. They exhibit the servant's heart of Christ who ran from heaven so that He could run the human race alongside us."

"Strength is a place deep within your soul where fear is replaced with a relentless pursuit to glorify God by doing more than you ever thought possible!"

"My journey is by faith. My hope is in my Savior, Jesus Christ. May my every word and action give glory to the ONE who rescued me -- who is my Savior -- who lifted me up through His love, mercy, and grace! He has set me free -- I am redeemed!"

GRACE-NOTES

GRACE-NOTES

GRACE-NOTES

GRACE-NOTES

GRACE-NOTES

GRACE-NOTES

ABOUT THE AUTHOR

From one t-shirt to the largest ministry for endurance athletes in the world – Chris Gillespie calls TEAM 413 a miracle of God's grace. In 2003 Gillespie founded the non-profit ministry inspired by God's calling in his life. Even though he has had a very successful professional career in sports medicine, TEAM 413 is his passion – a labor of love for runners and other endurance athletes worldwide. Whether challenging others to walk a lap around a track or run a mile, change an attitude or improve a relationship, Gillespie shares a message of hope, confidence, perseverance, courage, and strength. His ultimate goal is to exhibit in his own life and to impart to others the truth of his life verse, Philippians 4:13 – "I can do all things through Christ who strengthens me."

A 35-year veteran in the field of athletic training, Chris was inducted into the Alabama Athletic Trainers' Association Hall of Fame in 2002 and the Southeast Athletic Trainers' Association Hall of Fame in 2008. The highest honor of his stellar career came in June 2012 when he was inducted into the National Athletic Trainers' Association Hall of Fame, an honor that exists to recognize the very best in the profession of athletic training.

A native of Pontotoc, Mississippi, Chris and his wife, Kiki, now live in Seacrest, Florida. Chris has two daughters, Morgan and Ashley and two step children, Gerrit and Hanna.

ORDERING GRACE-WORDS

If GRACE-WORDS touched your heart and you would like to display one of them in your home, office, or give one as a gift — we offer individual prints at $10.00 each plus shipping. Contact kiki@team413.org for additional information.

AUTHOR CONTACT INFORMATION

Chris A. Gillespie
TEAM 413 – GRACERUNNER MINISTRIES
268 Seabreeze Court
Seacrest, FL 32413

www.team413.org